EXPLORING AUSTRALIA

EXPLORING AUSTRALIA

AURORA WINTERS

CONTENTS

CHAPTER 1

Introduction

Australia is a vast and mysterious island - a land of staggering contrast and beauty, including the desolate expanse of the Outback wilderness, the mountain ranges, the lush and magnificent Great Barrier Reef, the rainforest and rainforest waterfalls, famous surf-pounded beaches, and the icons of the Sydney Harbor. The sheer scale is almost beyond belief. Australia's indigenous Aboriginal tribes have been living on the island for at least 40,000 years, long before the first European settlers arrived in the late 18th century. The continent's European history has been primarily British, and for many years Australia was a penal colony for British convicts. Today, the rugged island of Australia lies at the crossroads of the Pacific and Indian Oceans.

The climate varies from tropical in the north to cool temperate in the south and much of the interior is hot and dry in summer. It is the sixth largest country in the world in terms of land mass. The country also has a large wine industry and is a major producer of gold, as well as the site of an enormous mining boom. As visitors know, Australia enjoys a multitude of pristine beaches and is the home to many fantastical creatures - kangaroos, koalas, platypuses, and wombats on land, and sharks, crocodiles, turtles, and abalone in the sea. Perhaps one of the best things about Australia is the sense of space. It's large enough to allow exploration and personal discovery, to come into contact with unique wildlife, and to enjoy a wide variety of outdoor activities, such as walks, tours, adventures, and wildlife encounters. For gourmet lovers or food tourists, Australian cuisine is international and one of the world's most distinctive, which has been shaped over time by waves of migrants.

CHAPTER 2

Geography of Australia

Australia is an island located in the southern hemisphere with an area of 7,682,300 square kilometers. It is the world's sixth-largest country and has a current population of 25.2 million people. Approximately 60 percent of the population resides on the Australian continent, with the remainder living in the various Pacific island territories or in other countries. The capital city of Australia is Canberra. The Commonwealth of Australia Act established Australia on January 1, 1901, and the country is in the process of defining its new identity. The Aboriginal people, who arrived in Australia 50,000 to 70,000 years ago, were the first recorded inhabitants. The Dutch reported the discovery of Australia in 1606, and in 1770, Captain Cook, while sailing for England, claimed the continent for the English.

Australia is the flattest, driest, and smallest of the earth's continents. Deserts cover 18 percent of the continent, and these, together with the irregular rainfall, place significant limitations on the development of agriculture. Rivers are often dry 90 to 95 percent of the time, and the fresh surface and underground water is the scarcest in the world on a per capita basis. With the exception of some mining communities, the entire coastline of the continent is one massive sea of aboriginal desert—quite devoid of human life or development.

The deserts are clearly one of the most impressive and stunning features of the continent, but they are also a severely limiting force.

Physical Geography

Australia is a country with widespread deserts, coastal areas featuring widely varying habitats. Due to its diverse geographical and climatic range, Australia is an attractive place for tourists and can offer conditions and attractions to suit tourists with a range of hobbies and interests. The west coast of Australia has some of the best diving spots in the world. This area is home to diverse marine life. These are natural dive sites with few man-made artifacts. Visitors can view coral gardens and swim through caves. The inland areas of Australia are harsh and wild, with clay ranges, gravel flats, and deep red dirt, replete with the scent of eucalyptus. These areas feature some of the world's most varied natural rock formations.

The southwest coast has attractive, clean beaches and high rugged cliffs. The south is popular with tourists who are avid nature-lovers. The fauna and flora are unique, featuring no less than 8000 plant species, most of which are rare and endangered. The area's natural parks are home to animals not commonly found in other parts of Australia. The east coast is most suitable for young travelers and backpackers or those who wish to engage in water sports, such as boating and fishing. This is the most popular tourist area and offers pristine beaches and an ever-changing marine life. The ocean in this part of Australia is full of life. The northeast coast has beautiful green islands, which are particularly attractive for those who love to sunbathe and swim. The animals here are diverse, and visitors have the opportunity to interact with interesting species, such as the koala, which are unfamiliar to many. The northwest coast is unique, with so much to offer tourists. Wildlife is varied and includes kangaroos, emus, wallabies, reptiles, and the world's smallest kangaroo.

Some of the best cave attractions are located here, and the area is famous for its underground fossils. These are major tourist attractions, and visitors travel to see these ancient marine creatures. Other amazing attractions include pools, which are carved into the rocks by water flow, and the Blowholes, which are situated right on the coast. The Great Barrier Reef of Australia is one of the most representative marine ecosystems in the world, home to a myriad of marine life. Its fascinating marine environment attracts many tourists to go snorkeling and diving. Enjoying Australia's great outdoors promotes relaxation, and tours are suitable for people of all ages.

Climate and Weather

Australia has a unique climate due to a variety of factors. Its great size endows it with several geographical features that in turn have a great impact on its climate and consequently its weather. First and foremost, it extends to the very edge of the Southern Hemisphere and is the world's fifth largest country. From north to south, there is a drop in temperature, and this variation determines differences in the type of climate to be found.

Looking at global maps that show prevailing wind patterns and the direction of circular tropical storms, the equatorial regions on both sides of the Indian Ocean are drenched with considerable quantities of rain. Australia, on the other hand, with little precipitation, is very hot from October to March with very little wind. It is only in April that the rain-producing winds appear, and that is when the north of Australia starts becoming wet. The drop in temperature during the winter months stems from predominant winds that come from the north and from the Pacific Ocean, devoid of any excess moisture. In the southern region, however, the winds are less intense, thus allowing the formation of large anticyclones and more rain. It is these types of variations that provoke an enormous range of constantly changing weather patterns throughout the entire country.

CHAPTER 3

Indigenous Peoples of Australia

Australia is one of the ancient lands of our planet. For about 50,000 years, or some say much longer, indigenous peoples fought to survive in an often harsh environment. Imagine people living here at the same time as the last Neanderthals in Europe or the Ice Age animals in North America. The inheritance of this ancient land is held in common by over 200 different clans and language groups. 'Indigenous' is the respectful term most people now use to refer to the original inhabitants of a country. In Australia, the people are called 'Aboriginal and Torres Strait Islander' - the term applying to the generations before the arrival of the first Europeans. Today, laws and cultural pride struggle to blend the two distinct cultures so that the ancient traditions can live with the new.

For thousands of years, the peoples developed different lifestyles and cultures to match their locality. The physical beauty of Australia was matched by the spiritual dimension of the Indigenous peoples. Their 'Dreaming' stories provide an ancient record of the 24,000 plant species, and the more than 750 bird species and 4,000 varieties of fish, reptiles and mammals recorded by settlers since the first European settlement. These anthropomorphic tales tell of how the physical features of the land and its inhabitants were created by Divine Spirits in the time of the Earth's beginning. Through these simple yet powerful images, the people gained practical knowledge of the environment, adding to their spiritual harmony with the land.

History and Culture
The history of Australia is a long one, beginning many thousands of years ago when the people known as Aborigines arrived on the continent. Throughout the world, they are famous for their culture, for their knowledge and understanding of their land and its environment, and for their way of life, which has remained unchanged for generations. Australia's recent history began much more recently with the arrival of a group of prisoners from England, who established a settlement at Sydney Cove in 1788. However, it is the stories of the region's natural history that have proved the most powerful, and these are the ones that were to attract the first European settlers.

Since the arrival of the British settlers, the history of Australia has been one of change and controversy, as the country has developed into the thriving and prosperous nation that it is today. Australia has been a land in which the need for change has always been tempered with respect for the past, and a genuine affection for the unique and often lonely wild environment that has saved it from overdevelopment, giving it a free, spacious, and open character. This enthusiasm for bushwalking, camping, and many other forms of outdoor recreation makes Australia a paradise for the nature lover, providing the freedom to explore rare and unspoiled natural attractions. Even without setting out on a journey, every visitor discovers a very special combination of ancient, natural, and human history when they take their first few steps into Australia.

CHAPTER 4

Australian Wildlife

Australian fauna developed much as the plants had, in isolation from the rest of the world for many, many millions of years. The result is an exceptionally rich and unusual variety of Australian animals. Many are like nothing found anywhere else in the world. The most mysterious of all is the duck-billed platypus. This is a curious animal shaped and patterned like a snake and equipped with a duck's bill, bird-like legs, and a beaver-like tail. Along with the echidna, a prehistoric egg-laying mammal, the platypus is unique to Australia and is found only in the country's eastern sector. The kangaroo, the koala, and the emu have become the most famous of all Australian animals and most people's image of Australia includes them.

Kangaroos, wallabies, and wallaroos can all trace their family back millions of years. Today over 50 different species of kangaroo can be found in Australia. The country is the only place in the world where kangaroos and the larger version of wallabies call home. Everyone knows that the kangaroo moves by hopping and that these marsupials carry their young in a pouch, but not everyone knows that the red kangaroo can weigh as much as 91 kg. Kangaroos are found throughout Australia, but in greatest numbers in the great dry areas of central Australia. Desert-dwelling kangaroos do not require much water and get most of the moisture they need from the plants they eat. The leaping gazelle-like movement of the kangaroos is best seen at dawn and dusk when they are most active.

Unique Species

Its isolation as an island continent has produced in Australia a remarkable diversity of environments and unique and varied flora and fauna. It is home to species found nowhere else, such as the platypus. As a result of more than 40,000 years of isolation, when its first inhabitants were exiled from the Asian landmass, the Australian landscape has become the exclusive preserve of the highest proportion of endemics known outside of the tropical rainforests. Since its widespread settlement, and despite its obvious fragility, the mismanagement of its natural resources has been amongst the most irresponsible of any country in relation to its size. Almost 10% of the total area of New South Wales is either in a state of serious vegetation decline or in immediate danger. Currently, much of what remains of the native vegetation is found in the regions of lower land quality which have not been converted to intensive use, or in terrain which is beyond the physical capacity of humans.

Traditionally, natural resource management (NRM) is the management of natural resources such as land, water, soil, plants and animals, with a particular focus on how management affects the quality of life for both present and future generations. This program was launched in recognition of the fact that the term NRM should be attributed to the resources of the rural sector as well. Rather than mere management, the rural sector has ostensible ownership of these resources, and with ownership comes the personal or corporate stewardship of the land observed in much of the land mass in less populated regions of Australia outside of urban encroachment. The nation benefits most when rural people self-manage their land

and have the initiative to research sustainable management practices. In response to a growing awareness by the community that many of Australia's environmental and resource problems were a consequence of the inadequacy of past land management arrangements, the Natural Care program was launched in 1987-8 to replace the Rural Lands program. With the enhancement of land management and the monitoring of sustainable production values of the land, the new program introduced an increased emphasis on biodiversity and glossary values of which the unique species of Australia were a significant component of consideration.

Conservation Efforts

Conservation efforts on the Kent Group of islands have been primarily concerned with the persistence of one species - the Australian fur seal. The world's colonies number some 40,000. Approximately 7,000 pups are born annually within Tasmania alone and a further 2,000 within Bass Strait. Although seals were not subjected to the human depredations that so greatly diminished grasses, marsupials, and birds on the larger island, the animals suffered their own entry into the early nineteenth-century commerce. Seals are adapted to a cold climate, with their dense fur underlying a layer of tough bristles. Unhappily, for them as for reptiles, their fur could be manufactured into outerwear, so sealing expeditions were mounted from Australia and Europe.

It is a source of wry interest that 30,000 leather sealskins were exported from Tasmania in 1833. Another sealing era cluster of years was 1855-67, after which Australian fur seals were neglected like so many of the other riches. However, the world, coming to Australia in the nineteenth and twentieth century, returned to its earlier interest. The IUCN astronomical coefficient of endangerment - classifying an animal as 'least concern' because it is common placates no one. The number of Australian sea lions, for example, has dropped to such an extent in the Wildfile in the last two centuries that they are now a rarity. The last sighting of a single animal in Victorian (i.e., with 75% probability, in the 150-216-year range since the first European landfall in 1772) natives was in the 18th century, on Kangaroo Island two hundred km to the south.

CHAPTER 5

Australian Cities and Urban Life

The result of 200 years of development and often hurried growth, Australia's cities display an interesting contrast of old and new, and of grandeur and ugliness. Most notable in the cityscapes are the sheer height of many of the buildings and an increased focus on residential skyscrapers. Other features include the pervasive influence of water in much of Sydney, for example, and the unique style of the Victorian city centers, epitomized by Collins Street and the impressive Paris-end buildings of Melbourne. Contemporary Australia is as rich and diverse as Australians choose to make it, encompassing a wide variety of ethnic backgrounds. The contributions of these different groups have imbued Australian cities with the tastes, smells, and experiences of many different cultural traditions. Some traditional practices of the past, such as Chinatown night markets, are enjoying a revival.

The establishment of gay, lesbian, and transgender communities in order to operate openly and in safety has been an important step in the cultural enrichment of cities. Cities such as Sydney, hosting in 2002 the world's premier celebration of Gay and Lesbian Mardi Gras, are renowned for their gay-friendly atmosphere and communities. Aboriginal culture in urban areas has also seen positive developments, with a number of groups taking steps to ensure that the significant cultural and historical contribution of Aboriginals to Australian society is recognized. Over the last thirty years, Australia's traditional manufacturing base has been eroded with a similar decline in old manufacturing areas. In its place, a service-based economy has grown, and with it a change in the central business area focus of many towns and cities.

Sydney

Sydney is the oldest, biggest, and most exciting of the great harbor cities that dot the South Pacific. It is a powerful kernel in Australia's globalization process, but it is also a leading center of economic and cultural creativity that is giving form to a renaissance in Australian self-perception. Sydney is unique in the clarity of its environmental setting, the self-assurance of its formal and spatial identity, and the way that a refined European urban culture mingles almost seamlessly with the more bold and direct modes of expression unique to the Australian cultural landscape. The commodification and exploitation of the harbor, however, is creating a potentially calamitous and long-term environmental degradation. For Sydney to remain a symbol of culture and natural perfection, therefore, there need to be supportive policies that enable its people to make the right choices.

Sydney is, first and foremost, the harbor. It is smugly proud of it and, thanks to the bifurcation of its two most important symbols - the bridge and the opera house - it advertises the truth widely and gratuitously. That is less an exercise in self-aggrandizement than in self-love, because the harbor is an extension of the imaginary sexual geography of the beaches, fantasy lands the very thought of which can dissuade the weekend tourists from ever really seeing and understanding the details of the symbolism around which they herd. Like Florence defined by the profile of its cathedral or Manhattan shaped by its complex opera of the island, park, and skyline, the meaning of the empyrean geography of Sydney is also the meaning of the bodies which inhabit the paradise. Thus, the strongest affirmation of Sydney's harbor-ness is not so much what it is; but what it is not. It is the anti-New York, the opposite of everything that Hong Kong or Singapore tries to be. It is a holographic representation of space, light, and water in which time and sound play intricate and metaphorical games of reflection and ephemerality.

The second layer of symbolism in Sydney is formed by the play between urban form and natural landscape with Mount Druitt, Bondi Beach at one end of two potent scales. Because there is Manglo Mountain and Narrabeen Man-made Lake, only by the presence of water in large enough bodies sense of masterpiece. First, it is not the water that gently flows into the city fabric. They are of such a scale and power that one cannot measure Sydney's coastline in the way we would measure a beach by walking alongside a compact group of towers. Rather, one must embrace the city and the beach in a holistic 360-degree survey that is revealed from the sky or from the high relief on a cliff looking down on the whole urban landscape in which water plays such an intimate and powerful role. Unlike Haiti, in which Cap Haitien, city and harbor are separate entities with mostly unexplored waters in between, or even Acapulco in Mexico, in which the brilliant arc of the Pacific beach is enhanced but not enveloped by the geography, Sydney is part of a unified harbor-landscape in which the water is the shared public domain of all its people. Second, it is not the sheer linearity of a Miami or of a San Juan in Puerto Rico with lines of pearly tower flanking the beaches.

Melbourne

Melbourne presents a seductive blend of architectural history, modern passion, and undying human spirit. While there are very few isolated tourist attractions in Melbourne, the city manages to engage the visitor, ensuring that pleasing discoveries are at hand regardless of where one's footfalls land. Whether one fancies colonial buildings or funky new structures, street art or gentrified shopping strips, enjoying a leisurely stroll or participating in any number of outdoor activities, inhaling aromas at a delightful neighborhood café or dining on multikulti cuisine – it is all here in Melbourne. The visitor cannot escape the pizzazz of Melbourne's reality. Few urban environments can celebrate its history and embrace modernism as does Melbourne. Whether the architectural marvels of the Victorian Era, the modern designs of the present century, or indeed, unveiled as part of current reconstruction entities, the architecture in the city is a nod to the surrounding history as if it were asking spectators to "sit and take a look".

Federation Square is "Australia's architectural icon of the 21st century". The square is not just buildings constructed of glass, metal and sandstone; it is about art, new technology, history, commerce, public functions, and about including every one of Melbourne's ethnic communities in the life of the city. The result is a very successful square with an extraordinary mix of buildings. It is hard to imagine now, but some thirty years ago, Federation Square stood as an unremarkable part of Melbourne – a "warm and windy wasteland". The renovation of the derelict railway yards helped redefine the city and its relationship to its people and visitors. Like the city itself, the design of the site did not shy away from voicing a history that contained sadness and decay mingled with grandeur and achievement. The present form, composed of a multitude of buildings assembled into a kaleidoscope of color and form, is articulated by a marquee and vibrant square that is "an outdoor Piazza San Marco for Melbourne". Parade past the square on any day and the feeling of energy is palpable. With each new encounter comes the realization that the square has another dwelling to look at and discuss, and just at that moment, its sharp angles and vivid colors give energy and verve to the observed. It is not surprising that this square is regarded as one of the "new seven wonders of the world".

Brisbane

Known as the "River City" because of the Brisbane River, Australia's third largest city proves to be more than just a city. Located inland from the coast of Southeast Queensland, Brisbane is known for its perfect weather. The city is quite cosmopolitan while still reflecting its closeness to nature. Its consistent excellent air quality, because of the absence of heavy industry, proves not only pleasing to humans but also to the interesting koalas that occupy the city outskirts too. It was founded in 1824 and then established as a penal colony to penalize thieves that had been sent to Australia.

Well located, 14 miles from the mouth of the Brisbane River, which is sheltered by Moreton Bay, Brisbane has become a bustling, lively city. An extensive network of bridges criss-cross the river, which adds character to river cruising. We particularly enjoyed the CityCat high-speed catamaran that provided us a fun way of river sightseeing from the river at very little cost. However, a more relaxed, sedate cruise can be planned aboard one of the many larger pleasure craft that leave from various parts of the city on day-long trips to the bay and its 42 miles of golden beaches or neighboring offshore islands. Huge passenger liners can dock near the city at the new terminal near our waterfront hotel.

CHAPTER 6

Australian Outback

The Australian Outback is a place of heroic human endeavor, outlandish endeavor, otherworldly dreams and nightmares, and extraordinary survival. The Outback inspires the exploration of the Australian identity and has a deep place in many Australian hearts. Australians also experience the country through their coast, while Australians have learned to live by the coast for the most part, there is something about the Australian Outback that calls for the human spirit to overcome alienating elements such as bushfires, floods, cyclones, and droughts. In spite of being such a challenging place, the Outback is one of the last great pristine areas left on Earth and international travelers are attracted to both it and to those who choose to invest their lives in working on the land despite these hardships.

There are many ways in which overseas visitors can experience the Outback but regardless of how you choose to undertake this part of your trip, it is very important to do your homework well before striking out. Needless to say, it is also vital to take great care when traveling in the Outback because it is quite a hostile environment. Several key rules include being well prepared, respecting local rules, and telling friends or police about your route in advance. If visitors follow the local ethos and etiquette, a beautiful insight into that local world can be achieved, and that look will be genuine.

Landscapes and Features

Mountains form impressive barriers and are also exciting places to explore, especially for winter snow sports. Australia has a number of mountain ranges including the Great Dividing Range that runs relatively close to the east coast, and the Southern Alps. The Great Dividing Range in the southeast is the third longest in the world after the Rockies and Andes. The Snowy Mountains and Tasmania's Mount Wellington are popular snow skiing areas and are also used for bushwalking, rock climbing, wildlife studies, and other outdoor activities popular with tourists. The highest mountain in Australia is Mount Kosciuszko which is part of the Snowy Mountains range. The southern states are known for alpine regions, and the highest mountains in Australian mainland in the New South Wales Snowy Mountains and Victoria's Alps. Not forgetting that Tidbinbilla Nature Reserve provides nearby access to environmental experiences in the region.

Dramatic landscapes surround us wherever we are in Australia, and many unique geological wonders have been added to the long-established landforms over the past 500 million years. The Nullarbor Plain, covering about 200,000 square kilometers of southern Australia, has thousands of great karst features in the form of over 500 limestone caves, fossilized right across ages in the year-old stratigraphical records the walls of the caves. Included in the ancient continent of Gondwana, is the flora, fauna and aboriginal history of the Australian geographical landscape. The Nullarbor Plain's name comes from the Pama Indian word for 'no trees'. The plain, Aborigine munch, with no geological basalt or sharp quartzitic higher rocks, sometimes gently sinking to 25 meters below sea level. Roads pass through this flat plain in a straight line because it is too expensive to be allowed to change this for geological reasons. Given the appropriate conditions, limestone can become a karst as it is chemically drained and worn. The limestone on the Nullarbor plain is 20,000 years old, formed by lizards and deep-sea debris from the seafloor that once covered the region. After the formation of limestone beds 25 to 30 million years ago, the continent again emerged from the sea.

Outback Culture

The culture of the Outback is a unique melting pot of characters and traditions, and is dominated by its relationship to the land and a sense of spatial freedom. Its character and values are derived from the general pattern of Australia's rural population, which gives it a distinct stamp. The Outback has a way of life that has a small, environmentally damaging impact. The population of the Outback make a real and worthwhile contribution to society and the inspiration and nourishment they gain from the vastness surrounding them cannot be measured in what they produce. It is a feeling that people in the crowded world of suburbs, in contrast to their neighbors of the Outback, can never know. In many ways, it is fortunate that there are so few who identify with the Outback, as it helps to maintain the sparseness of the countryside, which is so important a part of its charm.

The Outback produces people like these for the people who help the true Outback population to maintain their simple rapport with the land. The immediate social circle which surrounds many of the work of these people, who are essential, is also vital. Outbackers are not knights in dramatic terms riding in to perform an important but impossible task. They live out there—year in and year out. Jobs include anything and everything, and nationalities include a universal range. Amongst them, without oxygen equipment and electric gloves and almost indestructible morbidity, the function was. The function held a certain image for the agitators but was obviously below the standards of some, or so the well-used and disreputable look of the infantry placed in readiness against the sandbagged walls suggested.

CHAPTER 7

Australian Beaches and Coastal Regions

The coastal regions in Australia cover a total of more than 20,000 km and are home to several billion people. These regions, particularly the beaches, play a very important part in the quality of life for millions of Australians. Beaches and shorelines are dynamic and complex systems and are important environmentally. They form a very important part of the identity and character of not only residents of coastal areas but those that visit these regions also. For all of these reasons, beaches are quite an important focus for the WCP research into the understanding and management of the coastal zone. The CRC has 22 such projects identified.

The beaches of Australia, and the coastal regions also, are the most popular among the public. In terms of active recreation, the use of beaches for sunbathing, swimming, wading, surfing, and fishing are the major uses. The water safety, both in water and at the water's edge, is a response to these popular uses. The environment of beaches is under stress resulting from problems like beach erosion, vehicle use on beaches, and associated sand compaction, beach litter and defacement, and the quality of beach water.

Great Barrier Reef

Australia's coastline measures around 37,000 kilometers and consists of an amazing diversity of marine environments including more than 8,000 islands. Coral reefs are the most complex and biologically diverse marine environment, and Australia is surrounded by the best-developed barrier coral reef systems in the world. Covering over 2000 kilometers along the north coast of Queensland, the Great Barrier Reef is the most extensive crescentic barrier reef accumulation of coral in the world, and it is also Australia's most significant natural and their most frequently visited tourist attraction.

It is made up of about 2900 individual reefs varying in size from just a few dozen square meters to more than 10,000 square kilometers and is made up of hundreds of islands and cays that add to the surface area of the reef. The extremely complex reef structures are built by tiny organisms called coral polyps which use thousands of living inorganic animals in their enormous skeletal structure, which in turn form a foundation for the many other plant and animal species which form the entire reef systems. The Great Barrier Reef is home to over 1500 species of fish, about 400 species of hard coral which produce the reef's unique structure, over a hundred species of soft coral, around 4000 species of mollusks, more than 700 species of seabirds and a dozen species of nesting turtles. It is also one of the largest repositories of marine life in the world and one of Australia's major breeding grounds for marine species.

Gold Coast

As the slogan says, Gold Coast really is a wonderland, where the laid-back Australian lifestyle is coupled with the razzle-dazzle of one of the world's favorite holiday playgrounds. Where else can one find such a vast assortment of superlative attractions in a setting that is part tropical refuge, part wet-and-wild water wonderland? And if adventure is your buzzword, Gold Coast is just the place to find thrills and spills to suit every taste. The resort is Australia's top family holiday destination, and it caters especially for the younger set.

Thus the new and improved Gold Coast, where Space Age high rises and luxury ocean liners either compete or co-operate with fun fairs and Waterworld adventure parks. Even the latest addition to this party-hearty playground, the impressive new Jupiter's Casino and Convention Centre, fits perfectly into the fun and games pattern. But Gold Coast never forgets its past, and this existing way of life forms quite a contrast to this paradise of sun and surf. The Magic Mountain complex is almost a symbol of Gold Coast's new multi-million-dollar development as a fun-filled and well-equipped playground.

CHAPTER 8

Australian Cuisine and Food Culture

What makes a country's cuisine unique? Its own unique set of ingredients, which in Australia's case are among the most unique in the world. From snags, prawns, and lambs to kangaroos, emus, and croc, this part of Australian culture certainly is as offbeat and different as it gets. When it comes to Australian cuisine, its principles and concept are very simple. Use the freshest items and you would know you will come up with a dish or a recipe that is absolutely fantastic. Use the same concept for a traditional one from another part of the globe, and you can be sure that it is absolutely amazing.

When it comes to eating in Australia, 'variety of cuisine' seems to be the norm. Of course, the thousand and one Australian wine from a region that most people know of, Barossa, is also something that is certainly unique to Australia. But what most people should know is that only the equivalent of 3 square inches on the continent is suitable for growing grapes. Yet Australian wine is mass-marketed all over the world alongside that of France, Italy, and California. This is also an example of what makes Australian cuisine so interesting. And it probably is the secret ingredient which brings these uniquely

Australian foods together with that special something that makes it become the world-class cuisine it is.

Traditional Dishes

Australia is a blend of different cultural influences, and its cuisine reflects all of them. Even though there are some traditional dishes that can be found anywhere, food specialties tend to vary by state and region. Because the water from the surrounding seas is pure and unaffected by industrial or agricultural pollution, Australia's fish and shellfish are fresh and tasty. Kangaroo meat is even leaner than beef, so it has gained popularity with the health-conscious population of Australia, also because of a public campaign introduced after the Second World War to control the excessive number of kangaroos. The animals feed on wild grasses and shrubs, and not on cultivated crops, so some Australians consider their meat to be an increasingly attractive alternative to imported beef and lamb.

"Coat of Arms" is a traditional Australian culinary dish, consisting of kangaroo and emu meat. It is most frequently found in the Northern Territory, South Australia, and the Australian Capital Territory. Its name comes directly from the continuous logo used by the Australian Government, which shows the kangaroos and emus facing each other, and also because these animals cannot walk backwards. Another typical and traditional Australian dish is Anzac biscuits, which are prepared on April 25th and have caramelized syrup as the main ingredient. During culinary festivals, cakes and desserts with eucalyptus leaves can also be found, while the wizard of cooking is called Maggie Beer. She is a cook who uses fresh-picked ingredients that are in season to prepare tasty recipes that are rich in color. Slices of emu are served with fresh melon wedges, or parma kangaroo can be tasted on the excite with wild berry chutney and wattle seed damper. There are a big variety of interesting Australian tastes that visitors simply must try.

Fusion Cuisine

As a multicultural society with a long history, Australia has seen a fusion of cuisine that borrows from many different regions. Fusion cuisine is seen as popular throughout the nation with most areas having diverse "fusion" menus for everyday eating, such as Chinese, Italian, and other regional cuisine. The Marks have compiled some fusion cuisine examples given in mainstream Australian cookbooks. One example they gave is Tessa Kiros' cookbook "Apples for Jam," which is a tribute to her ethnic heritage and to overseas and indigenous food cultures, and to her passion for travel and food she has absorbed along the way. Some other fusions include Mexican/tapas, Indian/Italian, Thai/seafood, Moroccan/fish, and Mediterranean/fish. "Fusion cooking is a way of highlighting the vibrant, diverse facets of Australian food," Simon Bryant says in the Atlantic Group projects. He likes to put unusual combinations together and recommends cooking sea urchin in a garlicky, tomato-oriented pasta sauce. "Australia is ready for fusion cuisine based on the fresh, high-quality produce being grown," says Michael Stobart, owner of Brisbane's Viaduct. He adds that while the style was "not exactly traditional," it was a hit with locals and tourists and cited roast pork with prune and lemon oil and snowpea shoots as a favorite dish. As seen in the above examples spoken by actual dining and traveling experiences of professionals and everyday Australians, fusion cuisine can actually be spottable throughout the country.

CHAPTER 9

Sports and Recreation in Australia

Australia is seeing a surf boom. The surf is up because of an incredible shoreline, a great surfing tradition, a pretty loose lifestyle, sunshine, and a lot of room. But Australia offers sports as many-sided as its terrain. There are more horse races than in any other country, a surprising amount of rain (in the middle of the country) for good tennis and golf, and fine, thoroughbred fields for cricket matches beneath the Southern Cross. Rugby football smashes through the line every minute of the day while antipodean rules football is a completely wild game for two months of the year down south in Victoria and the other Southern States. The country is also a sportsmen's playground. You can go hunting, shoot a rifle, climb mountains, race cars, or shoot the whitewater rapids on Australia's many rivers.

Australia offers four major spectator sports: cricket in the summer, brought in 1877 by an Englishman who started a match in Melbourne and is now played on all kinds of grounds; League Rugby, which has an interesting record of being played in Melbourne and several non-League football grounds. This rugged game resembling the American sport makes big headlines and scenes when it is on and is actually the national pastime. The most widely admired sport in Australia, and also the most widely participated in, is antipodean rules football. This irregular sport is like eighteen games of ultimate tackle occurring simultaneously, and it comes along every winter's week throughout the 10 to 50 games of any state's league team. Soccer is also a good game, played by Australians but best played overseas. However, hockey is a great field title and Australian golf courses have an international reputation. Surfing might be the most beautiful sport of Australia because it combines sportiness with the environment.

Cricket

Sport, with a capital "S", is really only one thing in Australia; it is not drudgery at the local gymnasium or the 'burp' of air at the end of a long bus trip. Sport is the peak hour - 3 pm Saturday; it is when people get wildly, noisily involved. It is in sport that the collective excesses of an underpopulated country escape: the cackling barrages of disgust when an umpire makes a wrong decision, the endless discussions about the relative chances for test teams, the displays of male bonding on rugby fields. Sport is about telling someone else how to play the game - even if the game is watching the funeral cortege pass, seated in a bath chair, laughing hysterically, you are five points behind. It's a sin not to 'have a go'. The appetite for 'doing' is voracious. Good sportsmanship - maintaining benevolence in victory and sour grapes in defeat - is just good manners.

Cricket then must find its roots in such a climate. A game that redefines the word tedious for all time. Standing in a white shirt in the full glare of a Melbourne December day, looking like a feast for assorted scores of foraging ants; legs apart in awkward silence you can be tried and judged for not walking carefully with one foot out of bounds (The bowler). Each run scores less than a full cheer but a wicket will ignite night sky cries of 'kill the umpire'. Cricket is not a game for the Australian appetite. With one exception; every four months there's a party. It lasts for five days and, in restaurants, bars, streets, and back bedrooms, it's the major topic of conversation. Family shots are interrupted with regular updates and, at night, while the midnight rush hour rages, groups of people will still be found sitting up at garden parties, sipping a bubble here, tut-tutting over the selection of the final eleven. Cricket is the Australian repeater game; if it works once, that's enough.

AFL

Australian Rules Football developed in Melbourne in the mid-19th century. By the 1850s, cricket was the most popular and financially enticing sport in the colony of Victoria. Many of the game's administrators were public servants or auctioneers who had limited working hours in the winter months. They were keen to give their minds and bodies a more sustained workout than cricket would afford.

Each game of Australian Rules is played on a mammoth oval ground or one built in Australian capital cities, a stadium large enough to cover a dozen football or soccer fields. The game is played by two teams of eighteen men each, although the team who are not on the field at any one time seem to number virtually all the crowd as they hurl invective or abuse about the officiating at the match. Each team consists of two wingmen, two half-back-forward lines, two centres, a full-forward, and a full-back. These headings remain the names of positions, irrespective of the fact that they are utilized in the game no longer. None of its participants are capable of running to or walking upon the wings or off areas and, whether in the course of play or not, nearly all nineteen of the men on the field are fully involved with both defense and attack. At least six of these are engaged in their team's forward play at any one moment. The game is free-flowing, high-scoring, and fast-actioned. Its importance to the players and watchers cannot be overestimated. Since its highest league, the Victorian Football Association, changed its name to the Victorian Football League in 1897, Australian Rules has progressively become a less parochial and more national game. It is at the moment particularly encouraged in Queensland and New South Wales, home of the rugby codes.

CHAPTER 10

Aboriginal Art and Artists

Among the significant cultural legacies of Australia's Aboriginal people is a style of art that is unique in its associations to the land. To Aboriginal people, stories about their ancestral spirits' journeys and their activities during the Creation time before the earthly realm was formed are lived truths that must be maintained. To ensure the continuation of both the law and the Dreaming, singing and dancing are coordinated with the visual presentation of stories. Those stories are presented in a highly descriptive, almost geometric manner, which enables other Aboriginal people to read them.

Over the years, Aboriginal people have encountered overt and covert forms of racism as a result of colonization. There were political and social pressures against practicing traditional lifeways such that, for much of this century, many significant religious ceremonies of song, dance, and art were conducted in secret. The 1960s saw a political awakening among Aboriginal people that resulted in the repeal of some of the more upfront racial legislation. Though those relatively happy times were short-lived and the 1970s saw land rights campaigns frustrated and moves to maintain health and social welfare programs stalling, political changes did occur.

It is this increased freedom and cultural awareness that have enabled Aboriginal artists to make major advances in areas previously denied them, e.g., they have begun to create art for a wider market, and they have taken control of the marketing of that art via community art centers. Theirs is an enchanting, expressive, and distinctive form, an art that speaks clearly of the activities of the spirit ancestors and Aboriginal history as vividly as print or film.

Styles and Techniques

Certainly, there are many approaches to capturing the images of Australia in Melbourne, Sydney, and the rugged, arid Red Continent. The Australian Art/Wahroongha bookshops might offer some guidance. Not only has our journey taken us through the geographic wonders of Australia, it has also led us to look at other forms of beauty and contentment that occupied the minds of early and recent inhabitants of the country. The ancient dreamtime stories portrayed in ancient Aboriginal art could hardly provide a greater contrast with the vivid patchwork of an outback landscape viewed from a modern beige, high-wing airplane.

Books on the outback explorer Alfred Nottman and the era of the Overlanders have set down a rich tradition of the earliest adventurers and settlers. By the 1850s, gold had replaced wool on the social and economic scales of do-it-yourself Australians. The impact of the resultant growth in population can only inadequately be assessed in their art. Indeed, the pursuit of a scientist who converts his scientific approach to people into art and books is still continuing. His name is William Dampier, and he maps a string of Western Australian splendor. Our books even take us into the recent dirty political upheavals which Australia has now entered. When one sees the evidence of what is written from the time when the book was being researched, one can be in no doubt as to what the future holds for

Australia. Hordes of sick, bald, and wide-eyed creatures stumbled down to the water to bury the precious nuts in the muddy banks.

CHAPTER 11

Australian Literature and Film

Australian fiction writing has been overshadowed by its rich literary tapestry of poetry and drama. This is partly because Australian literature itself is, in terms of history, a young nation of not much more than 200 years, succinctly identifiable primarily in the course of events at a time when the North American continent was wrapped in non-event. Secondly, the men and women who have written fiction as part of Australia's creative urge, although they had the upper hand in terms of numbers and quality, have endured a smaller world of response in terms of demography to their efforts.

In the beginning, however, there were very few of them, and these were almost completely castaways and mariners. There was a scattering of prose - travel books and such, but in the broad mass of meaningful letters in its emergence, literature was the prerogative firstly, and overwhelmingly, of the poets and then the playwrights, most of whom were born in the Eighteenth Century. Their themes and evocative strengths, it need not be overemphasized, were of the land and people, and of the sea. What worked in their favor was that the common technically set forms of creative expression predating and dating the religion, such as literature, had not yet had time to be greatly enfeebled by the public. The number of readers amidst whom they strived to reach the receptive, then, was small. They, furthermore, had not really begun to migrate to, and settle permanently on, the continent and for the newcomer, it would be a decade or two before the selective breeding of extractive forces made their collective presence on the homeland aware of the antagonistic and constricting echoes which reverberated moodily along the circuits of immediate contact, submitting themselves as change.

Notable Works

Among the most notable musical works synthesizing influences from Asia are Synthésis III (1972) and Sudamala for Wind Quintet, Strings, and Gamelan (1979). These unique compositional achievements harness the unlikely mix of a symphonic orchestra and the gamelan, a traditional mallet ensemble. Instead of using them as mere coloristic effects and to echo a notion of tranquility possibly loved by the Western world's orientalism, Mong-Fong has shown the full musicality embedded in both ensembles. Of equal interest is a compositional dialogue between Mong-Fong and a Japanese shakuhachi player. Since 2000, he has written a number of works for shakuhachi, employing this traditional Japanese flute ensemble. Another significant feature of Mong-Fong's works is his heavy reliance and in-depth integration of Asian folklore, literature, and religion. Through a dialogue making four other levels in addition to the musical level, he ultimately achieves what is deep and universal in the emotional realm.

Several of Mong-Fong's works are responses to philosophies and cultural assumptions about life. Thanks to Mong-Fong's extreme courage in crafting his aesthetically moving and intellectually engaging transcultural dialogues, Mong-Fong Choo might today be taken as a composer who sheds light on the roots of human stories for his contemporaries in our advanced hyper-digital era. The ultimate music of Mong-Fong Choo is at odds with the actually suffering world filled with dangerous amnesia. This chapter is devoted to a brief look at Mong-Fong's musical journey. Moreover, Mong-Fong's unique contribution will also serve as a representative case highlighting the fertile ground for paradigm-changing achievements in the transcultural realm of music.

CHAPTER 12

Australian Music and Dance

Australian music and dance have as many influences and traditional attributes as the experience and character of the country. The first songs and dances of Australian's Aboriginal inhabitants were expressions of nature, performed to reflect the essence of the earth. Today, tribal music and dance is a poignant art form, expressed within the framework of the legendary Dreamtime. These dance performances are powerful visual displays which depict the Aboriginal understanding of the origins and mysteries of the world. They are performed within a strict traditional framework and accompanied by chanting and thudding rhythms of contemporary music. The rhythm and sound of music is timeless, transmitting messages of ancient myths and legends, as well as the happenings of everyday life.

The sounds of the legendary didgeridoo bring an air of mysterious beauty and ancient spiritual dignity unlike any other musical instrument. Believed by many to be the first musical instrument in the world, the sound of the didgeridoo echoes across the outback of Australia. This iconic music is steeped in the mystique that is the legend of Aboriginal culture. In contrast, the now-lost innocence of young convicts is captured in the charming tunes of the banjo, while the grand scale of the wind orchestra and symphony reflect the many influences and orchestration of a developing nation. The guitars of Slim Dusty, the crooning ballads of the late Peter Dawson and the recent acclaim of The Ten Tenors convey pieces of Australia's unique rhythm and sound. Today, a vibrant world of musical composition thrives, expressing the character and experience of contemporary life in Australia. With a musical culture that reflects the modern spirit of a nation, it is not surprising that Australian music has been instrumental in influencing some of the world's most acclaimed contemporary talents.

Influential Artists

There were few professional artists in these early years, so those who did take up the brush recorded a particular set of views. John Eyre's book The State of the Colony in South Australia concentrated on these and turned a critical spotlight on the colony's development. Eyre's sketches tell a unique story and provide us with some of the few accurate depictions of the area at such an early time. S.T. Gill, the colonial itinerant artist, is notorious for his portrayals of drunken, tattooed gold prospectors, as is German artist George French Angas. But S.T. Gill also painted picturesque views of pastoral Australia and of everyday rural and metropolitan life in the developing colonies which today offer invaluable records.

There was, however, a class of artists for whom the intrinsic value of the landscape was paramount. Tom Roberts, Arthur Streeton, Frederick McCubbin, and Charles Conder, together with other artists of this period, were the members of the Heidelberg School. Their inspired paintings chronicled the hardships, triumphs, and tragedies of the Australian bush. These artists began to paint the light, the open spaces, the heat, and the dust that make up Australia, and the response of the Australian public to this real, visual record provided a nation's pride and confidence. During the 1920s, when Australia went through a national explosion of creativity, setting the trend for the forming of a truly Australian cinema and a national literature, we also bore witness to the birth of modernism in our visual arts. In Australia, the driving force in modern art was the migrant artist Roy de Maistre. Along with Frank and Margel Hinder, Ralph Balson, and Grace Crowley, he sought to find an original visual language as a response to changing contemporary modes of thought in all intellectual fields.

CHAPTER 13

Australian Festivals and Events

Australia is known for its many festivals and special occasions. Ranging from cultural to sporting to just plain weird, there's sure to be something on at almost any time of the year in most settings. As with many other services, most of the larger street press and entertainment guides can be a good source of current information - you can find these at hostels, cafes, bars, shops or even the street. State and territory tourist organizations also tend to have regular electronic newsletters detailing events in that state. A really good resource that you may come across in the myriad of promotional material is a book called "Festival City: An Australian guide to carnivals and celebrations" published by Picador. It outlines over 200 of Australia's best festivals.

New Year's Eve, or simply "New Year", occurs on 31 December and commemorates the start of the year. The Sydney New Year's Eve celebrations are the most famous, beginning at 8:30 pm with the family-oriented fireworks displays. At midnight, the main fireworks go off, and the loud bangs echo across the city. People head out to local dance bars or clubs, or perhaps live music venues where it is easy to find what is on. Crime rates tend to climb and the police service is always on full alert, offering increased security in the streets and on public transport to curb potential alcohol- and drug-related violence, RBT (Random Breath Testing) units and booze buses. Alcohol licenses are secured well in advance, and laws about noise levels and drinking in public are relaxed for the night, but there are still inevitably some incidents. At 1 am, all pubs and clubs are closed and in some cases, alcohol is banned from being sold on the streets.

Sydney Mardi Gras

Now in its 34th year, Sydney's Gay and Lesbian Mardi Gras has thrived and grown from a personal political avenue to promote equal rights for the gay community in 1978, to an internationally recognised party celebration of pride and diversity that attracts tens of thousands of international visitors every year. From the first march of 1978, where more than half the participating 3000 marchers were arrested and brutalised by NSW Police, to a smooth running and user-friendly festival attracting serious A-list celebrities, health activists, pensioners, parents, and professionals to a packed 90 event program in 2009.

The number of events and attendees, public and corporate sponsors, and government respect and acknowledgement of the economic and social benefit that this significant event contributes to the City of Sydney over the past three decades has been remarkable. Because of Americans Bob Newberry and an appearance by Imagination entrepreneur John Ware, the Mardi Gras in Australia was born. Sydney's first Mardi Gras, named after the Sydney University student parade of 1973, was a self-conscious, visible celebration and assertion by the gay community of gay pride in the public arena. It demanded a change in the lack of legal rights and respect from the government of the day. By 1986, following the decriminalisation of male homosexuality and years of protest and reform, the Mardi Gras organisers were allowed to come in from the cold and wanted to clean up the law.

Melbourne Cup

Many travelers to Australia schedule their holiday so that they will either be in Melbourne or at an interesting place in the countryside on the first Tuesday in November. On this day, over one hundred thousand Australians and visitors from all over the world become entranced with the style and star-studded glamour of the Melbourne Cup. In every house, on most sheep stations, and in some of the smallest, back-of-beyond communities, people who have never seen a horse race throughout the rest of the year are taking part in a sweepstake on the Cup.

The city of Melbourne is deserted except for those who take part in the celebration of what many refer to as 'Australia's national festival'. Not really a national festival, it is labeled thus because of its old-world associations and the desire of both city and country dwellers to break away from formality and duty for a day of fashion, entertainment, and to the hard drinkers a little frivolity. The races are run at Flemington, a race course located on the banks of the Maribyrnong River, just a short distance from the city of Melbourne. In and around the grounds the sky is filled with helicopters and racing planes. Just because the horses are flying around the track does not mean the onlookers are just spectators. From early morning they are gaily picnicking on the lawns. The races are holiday events filled with all the pageantry and excitement found in England's Royal Ascot, only in Australia a pint bottle of beer is often substituted for the champagne. A track fence in the straightaway becomes a glamorous and expensive paddock for the who's who of Australia's celebrities. Women flutter about in their loveliest spring outfits, complete with magnificent hats, gloves, furs, and boots.

Horse racing - The Sport of Kings! On Derby Day, the Saturday prior to Cup Day, the ladies break out the furs; on Melbourne Cup Day, they display hats and long, silky furs; and on Oaks Day, two days later, they wear spring flowers such as daisies and roses, accompanied by sheerest veils and dresses. No less than a hundred and thirty-seven different fashions are represented at all horse meetings. There are displays in various store windows, and fashion parades are staged at some of the leading garment emporiums. Naturally, the shops do a roaring business during this week. With all those changes of costume required, they just have to!

CHAPTER 14

Environmental Challenges and Sustainability in Aus

Major Environmental Challenges in Australia

Australia is estimated to have lost around one third of its original vegetation due to human activities such as agriculture, urban and infrastructure development, and the clearing of native vegetation. In recent years, Australia has faced increasing pressure on coastal ecosystems as a result of increased urban development and demand for coastal properties. The significant level of threats facing Australia's biodiversity is putting significant pressure on a number of species. Australia's landscapes are prone to bushfires, but climate change has resulted in an increase in intensity and frequency of bushfires, resulting in widespread losses and placing a further strain on fire-prone ecosystems.

Australia has a diversity of landscapes and ecosystems, many of which face a range of serious threats. Popular databases compiled by non-government groups provided a list of threatened species in these various ecosystems in terms of intensity and urgency of threat. Many of Australia's marine regions and coastal ecosystems are under threat from urban development, run-off from the land, industrial development, and disturbance from human activities. The non-ratified Native Species Protection Act in South Australia has led to a number of extinctions of invertebrate species. In New South Wales, there is concern about the risk of extinction of invertebrates from forests proposed for logging. As with a number of native invertebrates in New South Wales, the original native invertebrates are under threat from growing changes to the urban landscape. The work of the Western Australian Museum has reported that a feature of the ecosystem at some of the 250 invertebrate species in the wet or tall karri forests of the southwest of Western Australia is that only 25 of these invertebrate species have been described by scientists. It is not necessarily that all species are still moving, some may well be new as they are described against the backdrop of large-scale habitat loss, ongoing logging destruction, increased fires, urban and infrastructure development, and a declining level of resources. Add to that the impacts of climate change (increase in temperature, increasing evaporation, expanding the range of most warm-adapted species, changes in the frequency and intensity of other species' disturbances) and invasion of non-native weeds and diseases, and many native species are fighting to survive. For many species, the only way to prevent extinction is through insurance populations at life-serving levels in nature reserves. It is important to develop the right suite of interventions to facilitate the future coexistence of humans, in all their diversity, compromises and seasons, as a necessary final step.

Climate Change Impacts

Australia is already experiencing the impacts of a gradually changing climate. These impacts are being felt in many ways, such as more frequent heatwaves, changes to rainfall patterns, more severe and longer droughts, more frequent extreme fire weather, and the acidification of oceans. There are many planned and existing developments in the southern hemisphere, and it is important that these are designed and managed to ensure that any increase in shipping, fishing, mining, infrastructure, and recreational activities are carried out in a way that ensures the integrity of the region for future generations.

The impact of climate change on southwest Australia rain-producing systems has been forecasted and includes a longer dry season, fewer incident wave cyclones in autumn, and decreased rainfall in western and southern areas. The increase in the incidence of extreme fire weather conditions experienced in the southern hemisphere since the 1990s and the discovery of ash from large-scale fires on the high ice Antarctic Plateau at an altitude of about 900m, in an ice core from Law Dome, has been related to drought conditions since 1847 and might be an independent test of southeast Australia climate models. The ice core analysis has the potential to extend the Ash Wednesday probability back to about 1850.

CHAPTER 15

Tourism in Australia

Tourism is one of Australia's greatest service export industries and also one of its most popular forms of casual export. In recent years, Australia has achieved competitive levels of visitor growth. However, in the very competitive world of international tourism, where both push and pull factors abound, it cannot be taken for granted. Continued growth and prosperity in international leisure travel require the tourism industry to be sophisticated and responsive to rapid international changes. Australia must have a tourism industry to meet the challenges of the future and that results from continuing our dynamic development.

The Australian Government does not invest in tourism merely for the economic value that it brings to the nation. It recognizes that it provides an essential mechanism for encouraging and maintaining international goodwill, mutual understanding, and global harmony at the most basic level of interaction that is human contact. In this respect, the 237,000 Australians who are directly employed in the tourism industry are in one of the most sensitive and influential businesses in the country. In meeting and sharing our nation and our people, tourists of today can become not only our best customers but our ambassadors of tomorrow.

Popular Destinations

1- Melbourne is a rich cultural city, possessing a multitude of theaters, galleries, and restaurants. Its array of magnificent architecture is partly a result of the 1850s World Gold Rush, coupled with a period of great prosperity which allowed for the building of fine public buildings and parks. Its flowering gardens, cricket, football, and fast motorcycles give it an almost European feel.

2- Canberra, the 'bush' capital, lies 160 mi southwest of Sydney and 340 mi northeast of Melbourne. Neither too large nor too imposing, it lies low in a valley surrounded by rolling hills, farms, and forests. Canberra is best known for being the site of the Parliament House and Old Parliament. It is also home to various national institutions and many other national treasures, museums, and monuments.

3- Sydney with its fine horizon, entices visitors to explore its many sites and pastimes. The famed city of Australia lies on a framework of systems integrating over 300 suburbs connected by over 26 railways. Circular Quay is the central terminus for the Manly and Sydney Ferries, the River class catamarans heading for Darling Harbour. The western line provides frequent services to all destinations: Cabramatta, Parramatta, and Blacktown in the west, Bankstown and Cronulla in the south.

CHAPTER 16

Exploring Australia: Practical Tips

Best times to visit: Australia is a vast country with several climate zones. The best time to visit the southern regions is during the southern hemisphere summer, from late October to the end of March. Winter is a better bet for traveling in the warmer tropical zones of the north, from May to the end of September.

Custom regulations: Australia has strict quarantine regulations. You cannot take fresh food, plants, or animals into the country. Milk powder for infant consumption, off-the-peg clothing, personal effects, and new items for personal use are excepted. There is a fine for individuals who infringe these regulations, and a possible prison sentence for companies. As a preventative measure, capsules are placed in the hold of aircraft to release chemicals in the event of a suspected quarantine infraction.

Time zones: Australia is spread over three time zones. When it is noon in Paris in winter, it is 9 PM the previous evening in Sydney and Melbourne. When it is noon in Paris in summer, it is 8 PM the previous evening in Sydney and Melbourne.

Electricity: In Australia, the voltage is 220-240 V. The standard socket is for a double-pronged plug. Take a special adapter for your electronics. The time when most tourists take vacations in groups is from mid-July to the end of August as it coincides with European, American, and Japanese school vacations.

Visa and Travel Regulations

Australia is separated into six states and two regions: New South Wales, the southern part; Victoria, the southern factor; Sydney, southeast aspect; Perth, the western side aspect of the region; South Australia, the aspect of the region, southwest aspect; and the area of east and north boundaries; and European Australia, the area, and the east aspect. The season, which Portugal has its complete summer vacation, is the best season for viewing Australia as it is in the southeastern hemisphere.

VISA Australia requires a passport and a visa to vacation for all natives. The correct credit score is given at the airports. However, if plenty of time is required, it does not apply at the time of flying. The credit score is needed to be used before you leave from the Consulate in fascinating Australia. As a visitor, 1835 of the official news reporters and corporate tourists are exempted.

CHAPTER 17

Conclusion

Australia has something for everyone, but only if you get out there and explore. There are exciting adventures in every corner of this enormous continent. Perhaps you will snorkel with a cast of thousands in nature's most memorable aquarium, or hike with a chorus of birdsong in the mountains. If all you see are the cities, you will not find her treasures: rocky red gorges filled with clear-water rock-pools, groves of eucalyptus trees crowded with lazy koalas, soft white sandy beaches as pretty as any in the Bahamas, tree-filled savannas filled with exotic birds and animals right out of the Jurassic age, vibrant coral reefs alive with too many wonders to describe, and every one of them is torture to depart as we leave Australia.

Visit the continent, race across the barrier reefs, scuba through the pinnacles of Ningaloo, hike and swim through the Blue Mountains, sail the Whitsundays, lunch in the glow of Uluru, escape where time stands still in the Kimberleys, count the sea-faring flocks of Cape York, explore the last frontiers of nature in Tasmania, feel the presence of joyous innocence in a very special region: Australia has something for every taste, but only if you get out there and explore. Only when I've made my last trip there will I be able to speak of a lifetime spent exploring Australia.